Test Book *for*

Wordly Wise 3000

Book
6

Educators Publishing Service

Cambridge and Toronto

Guidelines for EPS Reproducible Books

Written by Cynthia and Drew Johnson
Design and typesetting by Rebecca C. Royen

Editor: Jen Noon
Managing Editor: Sheila Neylon

January 2003 Printing

Name: _____ Date: _____

Book 6, Lesson 1 Test

Find a SYNONYM for each underlined word. Circle the letter of your answer.

1. She <u>bewailed</u> the loss of her friend.

   a applauded
   b regretted
   c embraced
   d denied

2. The Chief Justice dressed with a touch of <u>flamboyance</u>.

   a showiness
   b tastefulness
   c dignity
   d brightness

3. Two years of a foreign language seemed a/an <u>insuperable</u> requirement for admission to college.

   a unreasonable
   b silly
   c unattainable
   d minor

4. The meteorologist predicted <u>intermittent</u> rain throughout the weekend.

   a periodic
   b constant
   c unusual
   d driving

5. "Early to bed, early to rise" was a <u>maxim</u> Connie lived by.

   a saying
   b cliché
   c principle
   d advice

Find an ANTONYM for each underlined word. Circle the letter of your answer.

6. Because Harrison got most of his meals from vending machines, his diet was <u>destitute</u> of/in nutritional value.

   a lacking

   b without

   c needful

   d full

7. Hearing that the red team had finished the first leg of the race brought <u>impetus</u> to the blue team's enthusiasm.

   a an obstacle

   b credibility

   c a boost

   d energy

8. The anthropologist's documentary series <u>plumbs</u> the mysteries of love.

   a solves

   b ignores

   c understands

   d examines

9. Rebecca <u>wheedled</u> the car from her mother.

   a flattered

   b coaxed

   c gained

   d demanded

10. Abolitionist John Brown worked to <u>emancipate</u> American slaves.

   a liberate

   b free

   c enslave

   d release

Choose the BEST way to complete each sentence or answer each question. Circle the letter of your answer.

11. Members of what profession are most likely to have a <u>vagabond</u> lifestyle?

    a police

    b teachers

    c circus performers

    d grocers

12. What part of a lake will you reach if you <u>plumb</u> it?

    a deepest

    b warmest

    c shallowest

    d coldest

13. If someone's talking <u>detracts</u> from your enjoyment of a movie, the experience is

    a not enjoyable.

    b particularly enjoyable.

    c less enjoyable.

    d more enjoyable.

14. <u>Destitution</u> most often refers to people's

    a poverty.

    b sickness.

    c crime.

    d hunger.

15. Which group of people will most likely hope for <u>emancipation</u>?

    a farmers

    b foremen

    c slaves

    d laborers

SAT Sneak Preview

1. DESTITUTE : POSSESSIONS : :

   (A) lumber : wood
   (B) moisture : wet
   (C) rested : sleep
   (D) food : hunger
   (E) rude : manners

2. Karen extolled her father's — in an attempt to wheedle him into — her to stay at the party past midnight.

   (A) kindness … allowing
   (B) sternness … berating
   (C) generosity … neglecting
   (D) humor … forcing
   (E) intelligence … tricking

3. Although the widow's stern visage kept most of her neighbors away, Dylan was pleased to learn that she enjoyed —.

   (A) candy
   (B) gossip
   (C) visits
   (D) dancing
   (E) silence

4. The class's goal to plumb the — was delayed while they found a donor for the obligatory —.

   (A) tower … rope
   (B) pond … boat
   (C) field … mower
   (D) house … hammer
   (E) pipe … wrench

5. VAGABOND : WANDER : :

   (A) athlete : lose
   (B) musician : sing
   (C) waitress : eat
   (D) novelist : write
   (E) politician : elect

Name: _____   Date: _____

Book 6, Lesson 2 Test

Find a SYNONYM for each underlined word. Circle the letter of your answer.

1. They knew they couldn't go without it, but the hikers felt their bottled water was a/an <u>encumbrance</u> as they headed into the canyon.

   a tool
   b assistance
   c necessity
   d burden

2. International aid provided <u>sustenance</u> for the families hit hardest by the drought.

   a clothing
   b transportation
   c nourishment
   d dessert

3. *Wuthering Heights* is about Heathcliff and Cathy's <u>torrid</u> love.

   a passionate
   b forbidden
   c secret
   d happy

4. Michele took care to <u>array</u> the food on the plates.

   a arrange
   b toss
   c scatter
   d scramble

5. The ocean is <u>fraught</u> with/of dangerous creatures.

   a scary
   b free
   c sparse
   d full

Find an ANTONYM for each underlined word. Circle the letter of your answer.

6. T-shirts featuring the mascot were <u>ubiquitous</u> at home games.

   a common

   b everywhere

   c rare

   d annoying

7. From the dirty plate in the sink, Katie <u>deduced</u> that Jim had already eaten dinner.

   a guessed

   b knew

   c reasoned

   d figured

8. Clark was always the <u>laggard</u> on class field trips.

   a demonstrator

   b leader

   c follower

   d slowpoke

9. Bridget's <u>array</u> of snapshots was fun to browse.

   a display

   b design

   c order

   d mess

10. Inventors rely on their <u>ingenuity</u>.

   a cleverness

   b inventiveness

   c training

   d stupidity

Choose the BEST way to complete each sentence or answer each question. Circle the letter of your answer.

11. The <u>zenith</u> is the spot directly

    a above the observer.

    b below the observer.

    c beside the observer.

    d within the observer.

12. To say that something is <u>inexplicable</u> means explaining it is

    a helpful.

    b easy.

    c wrong.

    d difficult.

13. Which of the following is most likely to <u>encumber</u> a cross-country runner?

    a wind

    b mud

    c grass

    d shoes

14. Something that is <u>incontrovertible</u> cannot be

    a questioned.

    b proven.

    c believed.

    d repeated.

15. When people act with <u>alacrity,</u> they act

    a slowly.

    b reluctantly.

    c quickly.

    d incorrectly.

SAT Sneak Preview

1. Since he had always responded to her letters with alacrity, Denise was — when she didn't hear from her uncle for a month.

   (A) pleased
   (B) calm
   (C) worried
   (D) unfazed
   (E) ignorant

2. TORRID : DESERT : :

   (A) tall : mountain
   (B) humid : rainforest
   (C) dry : beach
   (D) green : valley
   (E) city : smog

3. Although the prosecution was haphazard, the — was incontrovertible and the accused was —.

   (A) evidence ... convicted
   (B) alibi ... sentenced
   (C) case ... released
   (D) judge ... acquitted
   (E) jury ... arrested

4. ARRAY : ATTIRE : :

   (A) arrange : display
   (B) adorn : cover
   (C) disguise : hide
   (D) reveal : mask
   (E) decorate : ornament

5. Although the trail was fraught with —, Shayne was determined to traverse it like a/an —.

   (A) signposts ... native
   (B) markers ... novice
   (C) rocks ... child
   (D) obstacles ... expert
   (E) puddles ... frog

Name: _____ Date: _____

Book 6, Lesson 3 Test

Find a SYNONYM for each underlined word. Circle the letter of your answer.

1. She <u>consecrated</u> her energies to/on creating health care for everyone.

   a fragmented

   b directed

   c wasted

   d devoted

2. My only clue about what was bothering him was the one <u>allusion</u> he made to/of his job.

   a reference

   b expression

   c request

   d invitation

3. Speeding in neighborhoods at night without headlights shows a/an <u>wanton</u> disregard for the safety of people who may be walking.

   a ignorant

   b unaware

   c immoral

   d accidental

4. The conqueror sought <u>subjugation</u> of/for the natives.

   a liberty

   b freedom

   c control

   d triumph

5. Tasneem <u>exhorted</u> her friends not to smoke.

   a advised

   b requested

   c asked

   d urged

Find an ANTONYM for each underlined word. Circle the letter of your answer.

6. Martin's mother worried about her <u>feckless</u> son.

   a careful

   b irresponsible

   c lazy

   d serious

7. He presented the corsage in a/an <u>stilted</u> manner.

   a natural

   b artificial

   c stiff

   d formal

8. The <u>wanton</u> kittens found homes quickly.

   a playful

   b merry

   c somber

   d frolicsome

9. Maureen found that the trick to babysitting was to <u>dote</u> on the children.

   a spoil

   b deny

   c pamper

   d indulge

10. Nathan's <u>pensive</u> moods never last long.

   a thoughtful

   b active

   c meditative

   d reflective

Choose the BEST way to complete each sentence or answer each question. Circle the letter of your answer.

11. Someone <u>implicated</u> in a crime is likely to be

    a victimized.

    b lying.

    c judging.

    d accused.

12. Which of the following least describes <u>dissemination</u>?

    a collecting

    b scattering

    c spreading

    d dispersing

13. "The <u>trauma</u> of being orphaned as a child" describes what kind of shock?

    a physical

    b moral

    c emotional

    d spiritual

14. Which of the following is least likely to be a <u>lamentation</u>?

    a a poem

    b a song

    c an essay

    d a statue

15. <u>Monetary</u> is least likely to describe

    a language.

    b money.

    c currency.

    d coinage.

SAT Sneak Preview

1. Although it was a — ceremony, Grandpa bestowed titles upon Kay's dolls with great pomp.

   (A) serious
   (B) lighthearted
   (C) dangerous
   (D) popular
   (E) important

2. TRAUMA : INJURY : :

   (A) hurricane : wind
   (B) tornado : twister
   (C) sad : cry
   (D) event : trivial
   (E) shock : emotion

3. The team lamented their decision to spend game day — despite the coach's exhortation to get plenty of —.

   (A) napping ... water
   (B) exercising ... souvenirs
   (C) studying ... ice cream
   (D) sightseeing ... rest
   (E) preparing ... sun

4. WANTON : RESTRAINT : :

   (A) soldier : duty
   (B) employee : benefits
   (C) suffer : pain
   (D) naked : clothing
   (E) magician : illusion

5. Although he was never implicated in the —, townspeople still allude to his —.

   (A) rescue ... heroics
   (B) election ... policy
   (C) crime ... involvement
   (D) restaurant ... meatloaf
   (E) game ... touchdown

Name: _____ Date: _____

Book 6, Lesson 4 Test

Find a SYNONYM for each underlined word. Circle the letter of your answer.

1. Barbara was a <u>punctilious</u> host.

   a sloppy

   b careless

   c rude

   d attentive

2. Natalie's stories were full of <u>extraneous</u> details.

   a irrelevant

   b important

   c necessary

   d vital

3. Aunt Edna had a/an <u>adage</u> ready for any occasion.

   a fable

   b slang

   c idiom

   d proverb

4. It takes several weeks to <u>recuperate</u> from/to a fractured wrist.

   a deteriorate

   b weaken

   c recover

   d submit

5. Insomniacs have to <u>contend</u> with/from many sleepless nights.

   a relax

   b struggle

   c assist

   d retreat

Find an ANTONYM for each underlined word. Circle the letter of your answer.

6. A <u>sedentary</u> lifestyle can lead to heart problems.

   a   lazy

   b   motionless

   c   sluggish

   d   active

7. Sam <u>regaled</u> us with stories of his trip to New Zealand.

   a   bored

   b   entertained

   c   delighted

   d   amused

8. Relations were tense with the best friends in <u>contention</u> for the same office.

   a   competition

   b   rivalry

   c   cooperation

   d   tournament

9. Woody preferred to keep his room <u>Spartan</u>.

   a   luxurious

   b   simple

   c   frugal

   d   restrained

10. His <u>wry</u> sense of humor often went unnoticed.

   a   amusing

   b   showy

   c   quiet

   d   understated

Choose the BEST way to complete each sentence or answer each question. Circle the letter of your answer.

11. Which group of people is most likely to enjoy <u>camaraderie</u>?

    a   neighbors
    b   family
    c   friends
    d   rivals

12. Which of these things would probably not be among an artist's <u>paraphernalia</u>?

    a   matches
    b   paint
    c   canvas
    d   brushes

13. Where are you least likely to find a <u>hubbub</u>?

    a   in a library
    b   at a party
    c   at a soccer match
    d   at a pep rally

14. Which of the following is least <u>odoriferous</u>?

    a   a rock
    b   a flower
    c   bread
    d   perfume

15. Which of the following is most likely to <u>meander</u>?

    a   a tunnel
    b   a hallway
    c   a stream
    d   an elevator

SAT Sneak Preview

1. It was Ashok's contention that throwing a great party had nothing to do with —, and he was a punctilious host who always regaled his friends splendidly despite his meager —.

   (A) fun … smile
   (B) food … home
   (C) money … budget
   (D) guests … kitchen
   (E) family … personality

2. MEANDER : MARCH : :

   (A) dawdle : hurry
   (B) shop : browse
   (C) loiter : trespass
   (D) bounce : throw
   (E) paint : stain

3. Despite the — of her illness, Noni is expected to recuperate quickly.

   (A) nature
   (B) disease
   (C) weight
   (D) severity
   (E) insignificance

4. Since she feared that the temporal world would distract her from her — principles, Kirsten chose a Spartan —.

   (A) family … pet
   (B) scholarly … apartment
   (C) active … budget
   (D) spiritual … lifestyle
   (E) charitable … wallet

5. WRY : SMILE : :

   (A) waltz : dance
   (B) smoke : fire
   (C) cute : puppy
   (D) sticky : glue
   (E) bread : toast

Book 6, Lesson 5 Test

Find a SYNONYM for each underlined word. Circle the letter of your answer.

1. It was a major undertaking to satisfy the cyclists' <u>voracious</u> appetites.

   a constant
   b anxious
   c light
   d ravenous

2. <u>Speculating</u> in international currency was Mitch's hobby.

   a spending
   b guessing
   c investing
   d profiting

3. There are many <u>impediments</u> to earning a college degree.

   a obstacles
   b bridges
   c distractions
   d dangers

4. Joseph Stalin was a Soviet <u>despot</u> who was responsible for the deaths of millions.

   a benefactor
   b tyrant
   c patron
   d pushover

5. Ms. Perera can always be counted on to give <u>sagacious</u> advice.

   a absurd
   b reckless
   c foolish
   d wise

Find an ANTONYM for each underlined word. Circle the letter of your answer.

6. Her <u>indolence</u> affected her ability to keep a job.

   a dedication

   b inefficiency

   c idleness

   d drowsiness

7. Politics had been a source of <u>strife</u> at the dinner table on countless holidays.

   a boredom

   b struggle

   c fighting

   d harmony

8. Rising property taxes threatened to <u>impoverish</u> the new homeowner.

   a diminish

   b worry

   c enrich

   d hinder

9. Andy made a point to <u>enunciate</u> his words.

   a mumble

   b pronounce

   c sing

   d project

10. Most state holidays are <u>secular</u>.

   a religious

   b commonplace

   c worldly

   d mundane

Choose the BEST way to complete each sentence or answer each question. Circle the letter of your answer.

11. Crops in <u>impoverished</u> soil are most likely to

    a grow.

    b die.

    c blossom.

    d thrive.

12. To <u>venerate</u> something means to treat it with

    a respect.

    b contempt.

    c fondness.

    d sympathy.

13. A <u>cynic</u> is not

    a suspicious.

    b doubtful.

    c skeptical.

    d trusting.

14. <u>Contemporaries</u> are of the same

    a country.

    b ingredients.

    c time.

    d magnitude.

15. Someone who is <u>callow</u> is least likely to be

    a skilled.

    b young.

    c new.

    d inexperienced.

SAT Sneak Preview

1. Zach is always cynical of his sisters' motives when they start — him.

   (A) teasing
   (B) chasing
   (C) helping
   (D) attacking
   (E) mocking

2. Although they were callow, the freshmen surprised the juniors by organizing their fundraising team so —.

   (A) effectively
   (B) sloppily
   (C) poorly
   (D) hastily
   (E) quietly

3. INDOLENT : WORK : :

   (A) hungry : eat
   (B) stingy : hoard
   (C) liar : deceive
   (D) gossip : rumor
   (E) messy : straighten

4. Despite her reputation for sagacity, Trisha never wore a —.

   (A) watch
   (B) belt
   (C) hat
   (D) seatbelt
   (E) smile

5. Thought the team started the tournament with the voracious — of the student body, interest waned quickly once it became clear that they were —.

   (A) opposition … winning
   (B) support … outmatched
   (C) wishes … talented
   (D) regards … losing
   (E) hopes … silly

Book 6, Lesson 6 Test

Find a SYNONYM for each underlined word. Circle the letter of your answer.

1. After debating for an hour, Marla <u>conceded</u> John's point that education was a benefit.

   a denied

   b admitted

   c insisted

   d argued

2. Jim is <u>dogmatic</u> about the benefits of a low-protein diet.

   a assertive

   b timid

   c unsure

   d open-minded

3. The witness was asked to <u>aver</u> that/if she saw a third person at the holdup.

   a ask

   b declare

   c wonder

   d mislead

4. The menu at the vegetarian restaurant <u>embodies</u> the chef's beliefs about good nutrition.

   a incorporates

   b represents

   c visualizes

   d splinters

5. Callie refused to be a part of the <u>propagation</u> of rumors.

   a absence

   b shortage

   c abundance

   d spread

Find an ANTONYM for each underlined word. Circle the letter of your answer.

6. "Stretch" was an <u>apropos</u> nickname for the lanky runner.

   a apt

   b inappropriate

   c suitable

   d fitting

7. The demise of the newsreel coincided with the <u>ascendancy</u> of network television news.

   a control

   b powerlessness

   c inferiority

   d superiority

8. She <u>imparted</u> basic cooking abilities to/from all her children.

   a disclosed

   b revealed

   c withheld

   d gave

9. Concerned parents organized a book drive to address the <u>deficiency</u> of books in the library.

   a lack

   b excess

   c shortage

   d need

10. Students were asked to prepare <u>rudimentary</u> outlines of their projects the next day.

   a mature

   b elementary

   c simple

   d initial

Choose the BEST way to complete each sentence or answer each question. Circle the letter of your answer.

11. Which professional has the least need for <u>oratory</u>?

   a   politician

   b   actor

   c   programmer

   d   general

12. Which of the following is furthest from the definition of <u>assess</u>?

   a   determine

   b   judge

   c   share

   d   estimate

13. Which business does not rely upon making something <u>propagate</u>?

   a   music

   b   gardening

   c   farming

   d   breeding

14. A person who is <u>deficient</u> in something has

   a   enough of it.

   b   not enough of it.

   c   too much of it.

   d   an excess of it.

15. To <u>sojourn</u> refers to

   a   staying somewhere.

   b   enjoying something.

   c   traveling.

   d   shopping.

SAT Sneak Preview

1. ASSESSMENT : JUDGE : :

    (A) preparation : study
    (B) promotion : hire
    (C) decision : choose
    (D) value : price
    (E) introduction : meet

2. Even in the emergency room having her arm x-rayed, Melinda refused to concede that — were a good idea.

    (A) wrist guards
    (B) inline skates
    (C) bicycles
    (D) trampolines
    (E) bandages

3. Rather than relying on commercials, the candidate decided to use her oratorical skills in — appearances to propagate — about her beliefs to voters.

    (A) television ... rumors
    (B) personal ... information
    (C) newspaper ... understanding
    (D) radio ... threats
    (E) comedy ... jokes

4. SOJOURN : TRAVELER : :

    (A) expedition : explorer
    (B) hospital : patient
    (C) professor : university
    (D) cage : animal
    (E) camera : tourist

5. Despite being —, proponents of the tax were so vociferous that they seemed to hold the — position in the meeting.

   (A) wrong … right

   (B) virtuous … upright

   (C) outnumbered … majority

   (D) quiet … minority

   (E) loud … moral

Book 6, Lesson 7 Test

Find a SYNONYM for each underlined word. Circle the letter of your answer.

1. Lisa became more <u>voluble</u> as she got more excited.

   a loud
   b chatty
   c shy
   d reserved

2. Marcus <u>deemed</u> it necessary to spend all weekend preparing his presentation.

   a suspected
   b imagined
   c doubted
   d considered

3. You can collect <u>exorbitant</u> fees for doing something everyone needs done but no one wants to do.

   a excessive
   b reasonable
   c inexpensive
   d expected

4. The organization offered a <u>subsidy</u> to researchers willing to study pond scum.

   a loan
   b plan
   c license
   d grant

5. Yvette <u>belittled</u> her contribution to the success of the project.

   a minimized
   b complimented
   c flattered
   d inflated

Find an ANTONYM for each underlined word. Circle the letter of your answer.

6. Paul expected a/an <u>censure</u> for being out past curfew.

   a approval

   b disapproval

   c criticism

   d judgment

7. The tree is <u>moribund</u>.

   a · growing

   b dying

   c ailing

   d recuperating

8. Alex was uncomfortable seeing <u>amorous</u> displays in public.

   a friendly

   b flirtatious

   c fickle

   d hateful

9. He used his bonus to treat his parents to a <u>sumptuous</u> dinner.

   a luxurious

   b extravagant

   c expensive

   d meager

10. Greg could not be trusted not to <u>divulge</u> other people's secrets.

   a reveal

   b conceal

   c disclose

   d tell

Choose the BEST way to complete each sentence or answer each question. Circle the letter of your answer.

11. Who is most likely to issue an <u>injunction</u> prohibiting something?

    a judge

    b boss

    c friend

    d principal

12. <u>Fateful</u> refers to something's

    a consequences.

    b validity.

    c truth.

    d luck.

13. An <u>ingrate</u> lacks

    a attitude.

    b gratitude.

    c manners.

    d friends.

14. In which class are you most likely to study a <u>motif</u>?

    a history

    b math

    c literature

    d science

15. To <u>expostulate</u> is an attempt to

    a manipulate.

    b convince.

    c dissuade.

    d dominate.

SAT Sneak Preview

1. DIVULGE : REVEAL : :

    (A) empty : fill
    (B) discover : find
    (C) search : destroy
    (D) inflate : breathe
    (E) tell : understand

2. Unless she learns to show — for the favors done for her, Kendra has no hope of overcoming her reputation as an ingrate.

    (A) appreciation
    (B) contempt
    (C) mercy
    (D) pride
    (E) humor

3. MORIBUND : HEALTH : :

    (A) emollient : moisture
    (B) lively : fun
    (C) exhausted : energy
    (D) spacious : empty
    (E) warm : cozy

4. Nicknamed "The Lone Star State," Texas has deemed it — to have a star — as a motif on many state highways and buildings.

    (A) forbidden ... challenged
    (B) appropriate ... repeated
    (C) acceptable ... suggested
    (D) desirable ... hidden
    (E) terrible ... nominated

5. Even though she was always —, Sheila was at her most voluble when the conversation turned to her favorite band.

    (A) friendly

    (B) funny

    (C) supportive

    (D) talkative

    (E) quiet

Name: _____ Date: _____

Book 6, Lesson 8 Test

Find a SYNONYM for each underlined word. Circle the letter of your answer.

1. Marilyn's <u>demeanor</u> was affected by years in prison.

   a appearance

   b outfit

   c behavior

   d expression

2. It is easier to renew your license than to let it <u>lapse</u> and get it reinstated.

   a expire

   b slip

   c disappear

   d continue

3. The Food and Drug Administration is the <u>definitive</u> authority about nutrition.

   a initial

   b likely

   c possible

   d final

4. Be careful not to <u>affront</u> your elders with offensive jokes.

   a insult

   b flatter

   c inform

   d suggest

5. Barry's habit of gossiping made him a/an <u>pariah</u> to those he talked about.

   a enemy

   b outcast

   c insider

   d friend

Find an ANTONYM for each underlined word. Circle the letter of your answer.

6. The five minutes after the last bell on the last day of school were the most <u>raucous</u> the school had known all year.

   a boisterous

   b serene

   c noisy

   d disorderly

7. When not studying or spending time with friends, Pat enjoyed his <u>avocation</u> of collecting first-edition books.

   a hobby

   b career

   c pastime

   d investment

8. It helps to be <u>erudite</u> in/of many topics to win at trivia contests.

   a ignorant

   b learned

   c knowledgeable

   d smart

9. Carolyn enjoyed guiding her <u>protégé</u>.

   a accomplice

   b peer

   c student

   d mentor

10. Her <u>adroit</u> handling of the racecar made it look easy.

   a clumsy

   b skillful

   c clever

   d adept

Choose the BEST way to complete each sentence or answer each question. Circle the letter of your answer.

11. A <u>militant</u> is one who is ready to

   a   debate.

   b   picket.

   c   negotiate.

   d   fight.

12. A <u>lapse</u> in memory will cause you to

   a   think.

   b   lie.

   c   forget.

   d   remember.

13. Who is most likely to be <u>inducted</u>?

   a   a president

   b   a mechanic

   c   a pilot

   d   a secretary

14. Which of the following least describes something that is <u>tacit</u>?

   a   communicated

   b   spoken

   c   implied

   d   expressed

15. What does not describe <u>crusading</u>?

   a   passionate

   b   easy

   c   struggling

   d   prolonged

SAT Sneak Preview

1. Although he had been a tennis prodigy, — the sport he loved very early, Ross did not want his avocation to become his — so he did not play professionally.

   (A) playing ... hobby
   (B) quitting ... chore
   (C) excelling at ... career
   (D) famous in ... downfall
   (E) practicing ... notoriety

2. Though he pretended he wanted no recognition, Jeff was secretly — about his induction into the Inventors Hall of Fame.

   (A) thrilled
   (B) annoyed
   (C) embarrassed
   (D) upset
   (E) humble

3. LAPSE : PROGRESS : :

   (A) sink : swim
   (B) shrink : growth
   (C) rise : fall
   (D) start : finish
   (E) resume : delay

4. RAUCOUS : NOISE : :

   (A) rumble : thunder
   (B) bright : light
   (C) rough : touch
   (D) leaf : tree
   (E) sweet : candy

5. With the abrupt lapse in — and the sudden chill in her demeanor, her tacit message that she did not want to discuss politics was —.

(A) activity … announced
(B) laughter … suspicious
(C) smiles … imagined
(D) agreement … suspected
(E) conversation … clear

Book 6, Lesson 9 Test

Find a SYNONYM for each underlined word. Circle the letter of your answer.

1. Radiocarbon dating is used to establish the <u>antiquity</u> of artifacts.

   a value

   b beauty

   c demand

   d age

2. The teammates <u>appraised</u> each other's performances.

   a evaluated

   b admired

   c polished

   d studied

3. The neighbors <u>reposed</u> their trust in/from small claims court to decide who was responsible for the fence.

   a withheld

   b placed

   c removed

   d lost

4. Dan used his biggest knife to <u>cleave</u> the watermelon into chunks.

   a split

   b mend

   c shatter

   d merge

5. Roger had a hard time identifying his <u>nondescript</u> umbrella in the lost-and-found.

   a ornate

   b unusual

   c flamboyant

   d plain

Find an ANTONYM for each underlined word. Circle the letter of your answer.

6. Daria took care with her guest list to make sure conversation at her dinner parties was always <u>scintillating</u>.

   a animated
   b lively
   c brilliant
   d dull

7. Detectives <u>scrutinized</u> the accident scene before preparing their report.

   a examined
   b glanced at
   c investigated
   d inspected

8. Music purists <u>depreciate</u> new fusion styles.

   a endorse
   b belittle
   c disparage
   d insult

9. <u>Synthetic</u> fabrics offer both advantages and disadvantages over cotton and wool.

   a artificial
   b shiny
   c fake
   d natural

10. A/An <u>facsimile</u> of the signed contract was all the banker needed to begin processing the loan.

   a forgery
   b original
   c replica
   d copy

Choose the BEST way to complete each sentence or answer each question. Circle the letter of your answer.

11. <u>Allure</u> refers to the power to

    a trap.

    b deceive.

    c attract.

    d repel.

12. <u>Transmuting</u> is most closely related to

    a balancing.

    b creating.

    c changing.

    d maintaining.

13. Which of the following is most likely to have <u>facets</u>?

    a emerald

    b pearl

    c band

    d nugget

14. If something is <u>impervious</u>, it is

    a vulnerable.

    b unaffected.

    c disrupted.

    d penetrated.

15. Which of the following does not describe a <u>quandary</u>?

    a uncertainty

    b doubt

    c puzzlement

    d confidence

SAT Sneak Preview

1. Although the locket was nondescript, the jeweler — Serena by appraising its — at a much higher price that she had expected.

    (A) disappointed ... beauty
    (B) surprised ... value
    (C) helped ... contents
    (D) pleased ... legacy
    (E) insulted ... worth

2. Jennifer was — with a sewing machine and could make a facsimile of any dress she saw.

    (A) a novice
    (B) clumsy
    (C) an expert
    (D) impatient
    (E) unfamiliar

3. Sean was always a — sleeper no matter where he was, as impervious to sirens in the city as he was to crickets in the country.

    (A) heavy
    (B) restless
    (C) light
    (D) inconsistent
    (E) recreational

4. BED : REPOSE : :

    (A) kitchen : food
    (B) car : drive
    (C) plow : farm
    (D) knife : cut
    (E) pool : swim

5. SCINTILLATE : DIAMOND : :

    (A) dull : polish
    (B) beauty : cosmetic
    (C) adorn : jewelry
    (D) reflect : mirror
    (E) exercise : body

Name: _____ Date: _____

Book 6, Lesson 10 Test

Find a SYNONYM for each underlined word. Circle the letter of your answer.

1. Tuition at certain state schools is <u>gratis</u> to military veterans.

    a conditional

    b costly

    c free

    d restricted

2. Volunteers donate their time without expecting to be <u>remunerated</u>.

    a paid

    b billed

    c charged

    d gifted

3. The community will be the <u>beneficiary</u> of the money for the botanical gardens.

    a manager

    b patron

    c donor

    d recipient

4. The community center <u>solicited</u> canned goods for the food bank.

    a requested

    b denied

    c endorsed

    d lured

5. Since none of them won the competition, the class <u>commiserated</u> together.

    a grieved

    b sympathized

    c distracted

    d gloated

Find an ANTONYM for each underlined word. Circle the letter of your answer.

6. The chorale group <u>garnered</u> several rave reviews at the state competition.

   a   collected

   b   distributed

   c   gathered

   d   earned

7. The paper recycling campaign had been Mr. Horowitz's pet project since its <u>inception</u>.

   a   start

   b   middle

   c   end

   d   duration

8. The surgeon had to <u>amputate</u> the fingertip to save the hand.

   a   sever

   b   remove

   c   reattach

   d   bandage

9. Howie felt <u>magnanimous</u> as long as there was money in his pocket.

   a   selfish

   b   generous

   c   giving

   d   kind

10. The bureau blocked a <u>practicable</u> exit.

   a   useable

   b   useless

   c   functional

   d   ornamental

Choose the BEST way to complete each sentence or answer each question. Circle the letter of your answer.

11. Friends told her "all things happen for a reason" so often during her ordeal that the sentiment became trite. What best describes the sentiment?

    a fresh

    b new

    c overused

    d original

12. There are <u>myriads</u> of fish in the sea. Which of the following best describes the fish?

    a scarce

    b abundant

    c rare

    d extinct

13. Which of the following is most likely to be <u>amputated</u>?

    a appendix

    b tonsils

    c tooth

    d toe

14. Which does not describe an <u>aptitude</u>?

    a talent

    b ability

    c challenge

    d gift

15. Which of the following is true of a <u>boon</u>? It is

    a welcome.

    b unwanted.

    c inconvenient.

    d dreaded.

SAT Sneak Preview

1. Since he always felt he was better at math than at English, Colm was — to discover his aptitude for crossword puzzles.

   (A) bored

   (B) angry

   (C) surprised

   (D) humble

   (E) disappointed

2. The baker was not usually —, but sometimes when he felt magnanimous he would offer cookies gratis to his customers.

   (A) generous

   (B) mean

   (C) sentimental

   (D) friendly

   (E) available

3. Despite his incapacity for — his own grief, Mark could always be counted on to commiserate when one of his friends experienced —.

   (A) fighting … joy

   (B) resisting … anger

   (C) inviting … boredom

   (D) expressing … loss

   (E) defeating … luck

4. MONEY : REMUNERATION : :

   (A) oration : speech

   (B) government : taxation

   (C) payment : work

   (D) escape : luck

   (E) school : graduation

5. Although she felt uncomfortable asking people for —, Yolanda organized a solicitation campaign that garnered enough — to send the band to march in the National Thanksgiving Day parade.

(A) money ... donations

(B) help ... favors

(C) time ... support

(D) advice ... backing

(E) input ... attempts

Book 6, Midterm Test 1 (Lessons 1–10)

Read the passage. Choose the BEST answer for each sentence or question about an underlined word. Circle the letter of your answer.

ABSOLUTE POWER CORRUPTS ABSOLUTELY

How did Maximilien Robespierre, a country lawyer devoted to protecting the oppressed and <u>impoverished</u>, come to <u>embody</u> the horror of the darkest days of the French Revolution? As a young lawyer in his hometown of Arras, he sought to "pursue with vengeful words those who, without pity for humanity, enjoy the suffering of others." While serving as a judge in 1782, he was <u>incapacitated</u> with despair at having to pronounce a death sentence. He found the responsibility of ending a person's life so <u>traumatic</u> that he resigned his position as a judge and returned to his law practice.

He was known to his <u>contemporaries</u> as "the Incorruptible." While he was known to be moral and honest, he was certainly not humble. He published pamphlets about his successes in the courtroom to enhance his reputation and <u>disseminate</u> news of his triumphs.

In 1789, the king called a meeting of the Estates-General to hear the people's complaints. Robespierre was sent to represent his province at the meeting. A Paris mob soon stormed the Bastille, a prison where people were jailed for their political beliefs. The Revolution was underway.

Robespierre wanted a new government, and spent the next few years making speeches calling for the king's execution. His speeches were long and confusing, but he was a persuasive <u>orator</u> nonetheless. King Louis XVI was beheaded in early 1793. Later that year, Robespierre won an appointment to the Committee of Public Safety. It was his first official position. The period from that appointment until Robespierre's death was known as the Reign of Terror.

Until his appointment on the Committee, Robespierre dealt with his opposition peacefully. With the power that came with his new position, he found that the guillotine was a fast, permanent solution to the problem of his <u>detractors</u>. He came to regard any challenge to his authority as an <u>affront</u> to France, which he served with such <u>magnanimity</u>. He perceived personal attacks on him as attacks on France. The ego he showed years earlier now demanded the executions of his enemies.

Earlier in his career he considered himself to be the protector of the down-trodden. After being appointed to the Committee, he began to consider himself to be the protector of the nation. The notion of the death penalty had once made him physically sick. He came to use it with shocking frequency, sending thousands—all "enemies of France"—to their deaths in less than a year. He believed he knew absolutely what his country needed, and he was not <u>encumbered</u> by doubt, pity, or remorse. At what seemed to be the height of his power, in the summer of 1794, his surviving enemies found the strength to arrest him and condemn him, along with a handful of supporters, to the guillotine. The Reign of Terror died with him.

Robespierre <u>cleaved</u> tightly to the belief that his actions were what his country demanded. His <u>dogma</u> and his methods made him the <u>despotic</u> forerunner to such nationalistic twentieth-century dictators as Hitler, Mussolini, and Stalin. He is remembered as the architect of the Reign of Terror. If he had possessed a little humility, he might be remembered as the father of modern France.

1. In this narrative, <u>embody</u> means

    a represent.

    b champion.

    c celebrate.

    d endorse.

2. In the first paragraph, <u>incapacitated</u> means

    a made angry.

    b made sick.

    c made strong.

    d made helpless.

3. When did Robespierre's <u>contemporaries</u> live?

    a before he did

    b at the same time he did

    c after he did

    d in a different time than he did

4. An <u>orator</u>

    a listens.

    b gestures.

    c speaks.

    d writes.

5. An antonym for <u>detractors</u> is

   a supporters.

   b enemies.

   c opponents.

   d hecklers.

6. A synonym for <u>magnanimity</u> is

   a deceitfulness.

   b meanness.

   c selfishness.

   d selflessness.

7. In the seventh paragraph, "<u>cleaved</u> to" means

   a ignored.

   b abandoned.

   c stood by.

   d endorsed.

8. Robespierre's <u>dogma</u> was something he

   a believed to be true.

   b believed to be desirable.

   c believed to be worthwhile.

   d believed to be wrong.

9. What is a <u>despotic</u> leader like?

   a kind

   b tyrannical

   c generous

   d enlightened

10. An antonym for <u>impoverished</u> is

   a modest.

   b influential.

   c needy.

   d wealthy.

SAT Sneak Preview

1. <u>Impoverished</u> people are

   (A) poor
   (B) oppressed
   (C) in trouble
   (D) outcasts
   (E) lucky

2. In the first paragraph, <u>traumatic</u> most nearly means

   (A) enjoyable
   (B) interesting
   (C) rewarding
   (D) emotional
   (E) empowering

3. What best captures the meaning of the word <u>disseminate</u> in the second paragraph?

   (A) announce
   (B) spread
   (C) publicize
   (D) cover
   (E) embellish

4. In the fifth paragraph, <u>affront</u> most nearly means

   (A) insult
   (B) threat
   (C) compliment
   (D) attack
   (E) joke

5. In the sixth paragraph, <u>encumbered</u> most nearly means

   (A) delayed
   (B) endowed
   (C) concerned
   (D) troubled
   (E) burdened

Book 6, Midterm Test 2 (Lessons 1–10)

Read the passage. Choose the BEST answer for each sentence or question about an underlined word. Circle the letter of your answer.

THE LAST OF THE SEVEN WONDERS

Of the Seven Wonders of the Ancient World, only Egypt's Great Pyramid at Giza still stands. It is the tomb of the pharaoh Khufu, and it was an <u>antiquity</u> even in <u>antiquity</u>. Its earliest history comes from a Greek traveler named Herodotus who visited Egypt nearly 2,500 years ago, when the pyramid was already 2,000 years old. With its <u>facets</u> covered in polished white limestone it shone like a diamond rising from the desert. Light bounced off its surface like a mirror, and it could be seen from hundreds of miles away, even at night. Although the reflective surface was stolen ages ago, the monument is still an impressive sight.

The pyramid is made up of 2,300,000 blocks of stone, each weighing about 2 1/2 tons. The sides are more than 750 feet long and all are within a few inches of the same length. The four sides face the four points of a compass—north, south, east, and west—perfectly. It is 45 centuries old, and it remained the tallest structure on Earth for the first 43. Scholars have spent generations <u>speculating</u> about how the huge stone blocks of the pyramid were put into place so precisely, with the <u>rudimentary</u> tools they had. Levers, ramps, sleds, and even space aliens have been considered as possible methods for moving the stone. The theory that the blocks were pushed or pulled up spiral ramps made slick with mud is accepted as the most <u>practicable</u> of the theories considered. Another puzzle to scientists is the question of how the pyramid was built so evenly, with evenly sloped and centered triangular sides. Some suggest that they measured the distance from a <u>plumb</u> line, while others believe the same ramp used to move the stones provided a level gauge of the pyramid's progress.

Despite the widely held belief that ancient enslaved people built the massive structure, experts believe that free Egyptians were more likely the workforce for the project. Every year when the river Nile flooded their farmland, farmers would come to Giza to work until the water receded. Some think they did it for the glory of Egypt and to <u>venerate</u> their king, but others think they may not have participated entirely of their own free will. They were most likely <u>remunerated</u> generously with food rather than with wages.

In ancient Egypt, all dead rulers were entombed with the paraphernalia of wealth, power, and comfort they might need in the next world. Many were buried with untold treasures, like the famous treasure of Tutankhamen, better known today as King Tut. The problem of how to protect the consecrated monuments from thieves is as old as the pyramids themselves. No matter how ingenious the pyramid designers were, they could not build a tomb that was truly impervious to robbers. Thieves in the 9th century decided to search for Khufu's fortune, and they found no trace of the pharaoh. Nobody knows what happened to Khufu's mummy and treasure. Some believe the treasure was stolen before that attempt. Some think the pyramid never held the riches at all. Still others think that the ancient wonder did its job perfectly, and continues to protect Khufu in his final place of repose.

1. In this selection, "in antiquity" means

   a in Egypt.

   b in the desert.

   c in ancient times.

   d in stories.

2. An antonym for rudimentary is

   a primitive.

   b simple.

   c expensive.

   d advanced.

3. In the second paragraph, practicable means

   a feasible.

   b unlikely.

   c complicated.

   d popular.

4. A plumb line is

   a level.

   b crooked.

   c dotted.

   d vertical.

5. To <u>venerate</u> means

    a   to flatter.

    b   to show respect.

    c   to embarrass.

    d   to threaten.

6. A synonym for <u>paraphernalia</u> is

    a   personal belongings.

    b   tributes.

    c   gifts.

    d   decoys.

7. In the fourth paragraph, <u>consecrated</u> means

    a   valuable.

    b   enormous.

    c   holy.

    d   tempting.

8. What is an <u>ingenious</u> designer like?

    a   determined

    b   smart

    c   lazy

    d   clever

9. To <u>repose</u> means to

    a   rest.

    b   celebrate.

    c   withdraw.

    d   escape.

10. In this selection, <u>remunerated</u> means

    a   charged.

    b   paid.

    c   fed.

    d   honored.

SAT Sneak Preview

1. To say the Great Pyramid was an <u>antiquity</u> means it was

    (A) run down
    (B) valuable
    (C) from an ancient time
    (D) a popular attraction
    (E) unusual

2. In the first paragraph, <u>facets</u> most nearly means

    (A) stones
    (B) sides
    (C) windows
    (D) jewels
    (E) edges

3. What best captures the meaning of the word <u>speculating</u> in the second paragraph?

    (A) studying
    (B) arguing
    (C) researching
    (D) testing
    (E) guessing

4. In the third paragraph, <u>remunerated</u> most nearly means

    (A) lured
    (B) rewarded
    (C) punished
    (D) bribed
    (E) motivated

5. In the fourth paragraph, <u>impervious</u> most nearly means

    (A) incapable of being penetrated
    (B) impossible to escape from
    (C) unconcerned about
    (D) frustrating
    (E) inviting

Book 6, Lesson 11 Test

Find a SYNONYM for each underlined word. Circle the letter of your answer.

1. Trevia has an <u>aversion</u> to/for cold-blooded animals.

    a fondness

    b warmness

    c opposition

    d attraction

2. Chalmers works two jobs to <u>defray</u> the cost of his education and avoid borrowing.

    a pay

    b defer

    c extend

    d forgive

3. Personal computers have <u>superseded</u> typewriters as the most popular tool for word processing.

    a dominated

    b subjugated

    c joined

    d replaced

4. The administration was caught off guard by the <u>furor</u> over the decision to stop offering the salad bar in the cafeteria.

    a uproar

    b silence

    c calm

    d serenity

5. The manager wrote the weekly schedule on a calendar so it would be <u>tangible</u> for all involved.

    a vague

    b understandable

    c indistinct

    d uncertain

Find an ANTONYM for each underlined word. Circle the letter of your answer.

6. Waiting until the last minute to register meant Terry had to choose from the <u>paucity</u> of elective options that were still available.

   a abundance

   b scarcity

   c insufficiency

   d lack

7. Dad tried to provide one last <u>idyllic</u> summer weekend before school started again.

   a calm

   b pleasant

   c carefree

   d traumatic

8. Among the <u>amenities</u> in/to the community were all the shops within walking distance.

   a comforts

   b detriments

   c bonuses

   d conveniences

9. <u>Complacency</u> is the enemy of improvement.

   a concern

   b satisfaction

   c contentment

   d calm

10. The formula failed because it was based on a <u>fallacious</u> assumption.

   a wrong

   b mistaken

   c correct

   d untrue

Choose the BEST way to complete each sentence or answer each question. Circle the letter of your answer.

11. What remains after an animal has <u>decomposed</u>?

    a dirt

    b sprouts

    c elements

    d bones

12. Which of the following does not describe a <u>facetious</u> remark's tone?

    a insulting

    b joking

    c playful

    d kidding

13. Attention to <u>amenities</u> does not display

    a manners.

    b courtesy.

    c aggression.

    d politeness.

14. Where are things <u>envisaged</u>?

    a in books

    b in the mind

    c in photographs

    d in museums

15. Which of the following is the least <u>porous</u>?

    a sponge

    b marble

    c Swiss cheese

    d cotton ball

SAT Sneak Preview

1. AIR CONDITIONING : AMENITY : :

    (A) ship : boat
    (B) camera : pictures
    (C) clothing : wardrobe
    (D) broccoli : vegetable
    (E) shark : reptile

2. Judging from the — that emanated from the garage, Teresa — that something had died and was decomposing under the floor.

    (A) smell … suspected
    (B) pattern … knew
    (C) light … doubted
    (D) traffic … thought
    (E) sound … considered

3. Based on what they had envisaged before arriving at the amusement park, the twins were averse to riding the roller coaster. After they saw the — the others were having, they decided to —.

    (A) ordeal … ride
    (B) fun … reconsider
    (C) thrill … gloat
    (D) scare … participate
    (E) trouble … join

4. IDYLL : PLEASANT : :

    (A) carnival : serene
    (B) event : joyous
    (C) ordeal : difficult
    (D) jaunt : lengthy
    (E) observance : somber

5. Although there seemed to be great interest in the concert, the quartet was — by the paucity of the turnout.

   (A) disappointed
   (B) excited
   (C) empowered
   (D) motivated
   (E) thrilled

Name: _____ Date: _____

Book 6, Lesson 12 Test

Find a SYNONYM for each underlined word. Circle the letter of your answer.

1. Marla found it hard to <u>empathize</u> with/for people whose experiences were so different from her own.

   a console

   b show understanding

   c pity

   d criticize

2. Since Molly was soaking wet when she arrived, Aidan <u>inferred</u> that it was raining outside.

   a deduced

   b doubted

   c considered

   d saw

3. Diabetes often <u>manifests</u> itself as a persistent thirst.

   a masks

   b hides

   c disguises

   d reveals

4. George's skilled artist's eye could see the <u>nuances</u> that separated sage green from moss green.

   a differences

   b gradations

   c similarities

   d colors

5. Though she knew it would never be published, Cynthia spent years working on her <u>treatise</u> on junk food through the ages.

   a composition

   b collage

   c play

   d speech

Find an ANTONYM for each underlined word. Circle the letter of your answer.

6. Cody kept a positive attitude even when faced with <u>adversity</u>.

   a hardship

   b misfortune

   c advantage

   d disability

7. Simon had a few <u>cardinal</u> rules for borrowing his books.

   a important

   b chief

   c major

   d general

8. Max's explanation for why the chair was on the roof was not <u>credible</u>.

   a suspicious

   b believable

   c true

   d reliable

9. After the detective described the nature of the crime to her, the psychic had a/an <u>intuitive</u> idea about where to find the money.

   a outrageous

   b practical

   c sensed

   d reasoned

10. Josh found the competition so <u>harrowing</u> that even though he won, he vowed never to do it again.

   a distressing

   b painful

   c enjoyable

   d unusual

Choose the BEST way to complete each sentence or answer each question. Circle the letter of your answer.

11. Which of the following would not be one of a person's <u>faculties</u>?

    a thinking

    b juggling

    c hearing

    d seeing

12. You might draw an <u>inference</u> based on what?

    a evidence

    b arguments

    c luck

    d disability

13. "Blue jeans never seem to go out of <u>vogue</u>," means that they are always

    a in fashion.

    b in demand.

    c classic.

    d casual.

14. Which of these is most likely to be a/an <u>impairment</u> to a quick vacation abroad?

    a fear of flying

    b hotel reservations

    c passport

    d luggage

15. Who is least likely to need <u>solace</u>?

    a a grieving widow

    b a robbery victim

    c a jackpot winner

    d a high school freshman

SAT Sneak Preview

1. Since he had damaged his credibility by lying before, the coach — Nick's excuse about his physical impairment and — him to participate.

   (A) believed ... allowed
   (B) accepted ... forbade
   (C) doubted ... required
   (D) received ... encouraged
   (E) ignored ... enabled

2. FACULTY : SCHOOL : :

   (A) inmates : prison
   (B) groceries : pantry
   (C) books : library
   (D) animals : zoo
   (E) waitstaff : restaurant

3. Although the journey west was harrowing, pioneers found solace in the idea that life would be — once they —.

   (A) easier ... arrived
   (B) worse ... stopped
   (C) perfect ... returned
   (D) difficult ... settled
   (E) hardship ... landed

4. Hannah did not know about the road construction and could not — her decision to take a different way home. She just shrugged and said, "Intuition."

   (A) justify
   (B) ignore
   (C) repeat
   (D) explain
   (E) doubt

5. The pernicious effects of acid rain can be seen in the — to the stone statues in the park.

   (A) tribute
   (B) damage
   (C) enhancements
   (D) dedication
   (E) path

Book 6, Lesson 13 Test

Find a SYNONYM for each underlined word. Circle the letter of your answer.

1. The song's rise to the top of the chart had been <u>meteoric</u>.

   a slow

   b indirect

   c fast

   d surprising

2. Taylor's <u>precocity</u> in/for music had emerged by his third birthday.

   a aptitude

   b intuition

   c reputation

   d enjoyment

3. The science club was thrilled by the lab's <u>proffer</u> of meeting space and experimental materials.

   a suggestion

   b offer

   c request

   d mention

4. To distinguish himself from his voluble twin, Brett tried to be more <u>succinct</u>.

   a quiet

   b wordy

   c concise

   d kind

5. Jesse faced the principal with <u>trepidation</u>.

   a dread

   b confidence

   c relaxation

   d anger

Find an ANTONYM for each underlined word. Circle the letter of your answer.

6. Jack grew weary of Bobby's always <u>deprecating</u> any new idea.

   a criticizing
   b belittling
   c embracing
   d ignoring

7. Try not to <u>discomfit</u> newcomers with too many personal questions.

   a calm
   b embarrass
   c taunt
   d perplex

8. Maria was careful not to trip on the <u>rift</u> in the sidewalk.

   a crack
   b break
   c turn
   d repair

9. Isabella's <u>overbearing</u> manner annoyed her coworkers.

   a pushy
   b submissive
   c domineering
   d arrogant

10. Getting a flat tire on the way to a job interview is particularly <u>untoward</u>.

    a favorable
    b unlucky
    c frustrating
    d ominous

Choose the BEST way to complete each sentence or answer each question. Circle the letter of your answer.

11. A child is most likely to <u>remonstrate</u> with a parent about which of the following?

    a bedtime

    b playtime

    c lunchtime

    d anytime

12. A <u>virtuoso</u> performance is most likely to be

    a funny.

    b boring.

    c long.

    d excellent.

13. <u>Blandishments</u> are not intended to

    a coax.

    b persuade.

    c threaten.

    d convince.

14. A <u>sylvan</u> setting is full of

    a animals.

    b buildings.

    c lakes.

    d trees.

15. Which of the following is a <u>solicitous</u> friend least likely to do?

    a forget your birthday

    b help you move

    c visit you in the hospital

    d cheer you up

SAT Sneak Preview

1. DEPRECATE : FROWN : :

   (A) praise : smile
   (B) congratulate : sneer
   (C) enrich : reward
   (D) compliment : gasp
   (E) dedicate : give

2. Good casting agents will — the blandishments of overbearing parents trying to — them into giving their child a role.

   (A) believe ... pressure
   (B) ignore ... coax
   (C) accept ... bribe
   (D) reject ... threaten
   (E) deny ... manipulate

3. Despite the old rift between the sisters, Jenna — the solicitous attention from Aimee after her —.

   (A) sought ... promotion
   (B) needed ... wedding
   (C) welcomed ... loss
   (D) requested ... move
   (E) disliked ... transfer

4. To give the children a taste of life in the —, the McGregors proffered their sylvan campground for a weekend trip.

   (A) desert
   (B) city
   (C) suburbs
   (D) wilderness
   (E) tundra

5. Despite Mei's trepidation about her performance with the symphony, nothing untoward happened to — her fears.

(A) soothe

(B) justify

(C) calm

(D) dissolve

(E) realize

Name: _____   Date: _____

Book 6, Lesson 14 Test

Find a SYNONYM for each underlined word. Circle the letter of your answer.

1. The toddler's vocabulary grew faster than his ability to <u>articulate</u> the words he was learning.

   a pronounce

   b understand

   c apply

   d recognize

2. Billy was determined to <u>decimate</u> the aphids before they ate his rosebushes.

   a nourish

   b kill

   c repel

   d embrace

3. Risk is a/an <u>inherent</u> part of investing.

   a unfortunate

   b undesirable

   c avoidable

   d built-in

4. The class was embarrassed when Ms. Wright caught them <u>parodying</u> her limp.

   a imitating

   b discussing

   c filming

   d noticing

5. It was hard for someone as <u>gregarious</u> as Laura to be alone for very long.

   a popular

   b bored

   c sociable

   d eager

Find an ANTONYM for each underlined word. Circle the letter of your answer.

6. Carla spent a month <u>amassing</u> thousands of signatures on the petition.

   a gathering

   b dispersing

   c collecting

   d accumulating

7. Roxana had never displayed such <u>pugnacity</u> before in her life.

   a passiveness

   b aggression

   c belligerence

   d rudeness

8. Jude bewailed his <u>reprehensible</u> involvement in the caper.

   a regretful

   b innocent

   c accidental

   d deliberate

9. Thanks to Luke's calling 911 immediately, the fire was still <u>tractable</u> when help arrived.

   a burning

   b destructive

   c contained

   d unmanageable

10. Rather than giving a straightforward book report, Clyde chose to surprise his teacher with a <u>zany</u> skit depicting his favorite scene.

   a clownish

   b comical

   c dramatic

   d funny

Choose the BEST way to complete each sentence or answer each question. Circle the letter of your answer.

11. With which of the following are you least likely to <u>garb</u> yourself?

    a bathrobe

    b shampoo

    c pajamas

    d shower cap

12. A <u>maternal</u> gift comes from your

    a dog.

    b neighbor.

    c cousin.

    d mother.

13. If good manners are the result of <u>nurture</u>, they come from

    a inherited aptitudes.

    b luck.

    c dedicated studying.

    d upbringing.

14. Which of the following is least <u>obtrusive</u>?

    a a bull in a china shop

    b a hose in a garden

    c a dog in a courtroom

    d a cat in a cradle

15. What does one use to <u>articulate</u> something?

    a pictures

    b words

    c gestures

    d ideas

SAT Sneak Preview

1. ARTICULATE : SPEAK : :

   (A) literate : see
   (B) wealthy : pay
   (C) graceful : move
   (D) warm : cool
   (E) colorful : paint

2. Impressed by Ray's dexterous skill as an amateur, the trainer — that the pugnacious youth may have a future as a professional —.

   (A) believed … boxer
   (B) doubted … bodyguard
   (C) hoped … accountant
   (D) thought … tailor
   (E) knew … driver

3. Charlie was a — guest. With his gregarious nature and polite manner, he was — without being obtrusive.

   (A) terrible … charming
   (B) delightful … sociable
   (C) welcome … rude
   (D) happy … shy
   (E) rare … obnoxious

4. SPY : OBTRUSIVE : :

   (A) panther : sleek
   (B) carrot : crunchy
   (C) benefactor : kind
   (D) clown : happy
   (E) miser : generous

5. Bob was a talented and zany performer, and his parodies of popular movies always received roars of — from the audience.

   (A) disapproval
   (B) confusion
   (C) disgust
   (D) laughter
   (E) anger

Book 6, Lesson 15 Test

Find a SYNONYM for each underlined word. Circle the letter of your answer.

1. Many long hours practicing were <u>antecedent</u> to Kerri's triumph at the tournament.

   a unrelated
   b preceding
   c coincidental
   d subsequent

2. Breaking her previous record by several seconds was <u>indubitable</u> proof that the sprinter had been training seriously.

   a unquestionable
   b likely
   c probable
   d suspicious

3. We gathered enough <u>momentum</u> on the downhill part of the trail to carry us up the hill at the end.

   a energy
   b determination
   c breath
   d support

4. Dark clouds represented a <u>potential</u> flaw in the plan for a perfect day outdoors.

   a growing
   b unexpected
   c unlikely
   d possible

5. Her mother insisted that Rachel begin to exercise her <u>volition</u> in everyday matters.

   a power of cooking
   b power of choosing
   c reason
   d responsibility

Find an ANTONYM for each underlined word. Circle the letter of your answer.

6. The divide between industrialized and developing nations is <u>accentuated</u> by the infant mortality rate.

   a emphasized

   b minimized

   c intensified

   d stressed

7. A classical music <u>aficionado</u>, Derrick had season tickets to the symphony.

   a detractor

   b fan

   c supporter

   d follower

8. Sam had a/an <u>visceral</u> reaction to the Holocaust documentary.

   a powerful

   b strong

   c mild

   d allergic

9. Melissa was frustrated by the <u>disingenuous</u> way Liz cancelled their plans.

   a awkward

   b insincere

   c indirect

   d straightforward

10. The family became <u>jaded</u> about lobster's delicious taste after a year in Maine.

   a weary

   b excited

   c dulled

   d distrustful

Choose the BEST way to complete each sentence or answer each question. Circle the letter of your answer.

11. Centrifugal has to do with something's relative position to the

    a   edge.

    b   corner.

    c   center.

    d   surface.

12. Origami is the Japanese art of making convoluted shapes from single sheets of paper. It involves

    a   cutting.

    b   folding.

    c   gluing.

    d   coloring.

13. What body part is involved in decapitating?

    a   the head

    b   the eyes

    c   the hands

    d   the legs

14. A masochistic person is one who enjoys

    a   books.

    b   sleep.

    c   exercise.

    d   pain.

15. If something is obsolescent, how likely are you to see it in use?

    a   very

    b   somewhat

    c   moderately

    d   not at all

SAT Sneak Preview

1. The convoluted plot was so cleverly — that even the most jaded reader — it.

   (A) resolved ... enjoyed
   (B) described ... understood
   (C) revealed ... finished
   (D) introduced ... dismissed
   (E) unwound ... believed

2. No matter how he tried to seem —, Claire found his compliments disingenuous.

   (A) friendly
   (B) threatening
   (C) sincere
   (D) knowledgeable
   (E) harmless

3. MASOCHIST : PAIN : :

   (A) daredevil : motorcycle
   (B) performer : applause
   (C) army : war
   (D) librarian : books
   (E) mouse : cheese

4. LIVER : VISCERA : :

   (A) milk : bottle
   (B) eggs : carton
   (C) car : motor
   (D) continents : Africa
   (E) smell : senses

5. Even though she could afford — appliances, Gwen — of her own volition to cook on the obsolescent wood stove.

   (A) modern ... chose
   (B) cheap ... had
   (C) fancy ... needed
   (D) sophisticated ... preferred
   (E) antique ... decided

Book 6, Lesson 16 Test

Find a SYNONYM for each underlined word. Circle the letter of your answer.

1. Dennis boldly <u>contravened</u> the school's directive about leaving the grounds during the day.

   a obeyed

   b acted counter to

   c supported

   d enforced

2. The <u>default</u> delivery method is surface mail; please check the "air mail" box if you wish faster delivery.

   a automatic

   b preferred

   c cheapest

   d usual

3. Banners <u>emblazoned</u> with team colors were hung all around the stadium.

   a written

   b pictured

   c decorated

   d described

4. Steven was nervous about his performance because he was just a <u>novice</u> at lacrosse.

   a substitute

   b regular

   c expert

   d beginner

5. Despite her age, Aunt Myrtle was <u>spry</u> on the dance floor.

   a stiff

   b clumsy

   c lively

   d awkward

Find an ANTONYM for each underlined word. Circle the letter of your answer.

6. To his <u>chagrin</u>, Dante tripped while trying to sneak up on Beatrice.

   a embarrassment

   b delight

   c annoyance

   d unease

7. Marc was in the <u>doldrums</u> for weeks after moving to a new city.

   a dumps

   b doghouse

   c best mood

   d basement

8. A Pulitzer Prize is proof of a writer's <u>eminence</u>.

   a power

   b averageness

   c prestige

   d talent

9. Richard <u>expended</u> so much energy preparing for the ceremony that he was too tired to enjoy it.

   a stored

   b wasted

   c used

   d spent

10. The coat was held together by a few <u>tenuous</u> threads.

    a thin

    b flimsy

    c weak

    d thick

Choose the BEST way to complete each sentence or answer each question. Circle the letter of your answer.

11. A <u>belated</u> action is performed

    a   early.

    b   on time.

    c   late.

    d   not at all.

12. Which of the following things is most likely to be <u>defaulted</u> upon?

    a   an obligation

    b   a loan

    c   a promise

    d   a tax

13. When a password <u>expires</u>, it

    a   no longer works.

    b   becomes public.

    c   gets renewed.

    d   must be reset.

14. Which of the following is the most <u>tenuous</u>?

    a   helium

    b   iron

    c   Styrofoam

    d   cotton

15. How well known is a <u>truism</u> likely to be?

    a   not at all

    b   a little bit

    c   somewhat

    d   very

SAT Sneak Preview

1. CALIBER : BULLET : :

   (A) truck : car
   (B) color : film
   (C) dirty : trash
   (D) size : dress
   (E) wet : beverage

2. Andre was chagrined to win the match by default, and would have — the chance to — his rival on the court.

   (A) preferred … play
   (B) hated … meet
   (C) avoided … challenge
   (D) denied … face
   (E) feared … tie

3. — that her work should continue after she expired, the eminent scholar left her fortune to her college for — research.

   (A) Afraid … additional
   (B) Determined … future
   (C) Eager … former
   (D) Hopeful … proven
   (E) Anxious … fundamental

4. Uncle Russ was an exponent of the sport of rugby among the neighborhood children and enjoyed seeing its popularity — over the years.

   (A) wane
   (B) fall
   (C) rise
   (D) lapse
   (E) disappear

5. TENUOUS : SUBSTANCE : :

   (A) poor : money
   (B) red : color
   (C) cushion : spring
   (D) strength : power
   (E) hunger : food

Name: _____   Date: _____

Book 6, Lesson 17 Test

Find a SYNONYM for each underlined word. Circle the letter of your answer.

1. Ms. Diaz's library was <u>cited</u> for constantly innovating.

   a noted
   b punished
   c rebuked
   d praised

2. While she did not claim to be innocent, the prisoner appealed to the governor for <u>clemency</u>.

   a release
   b mercy
   c favors
   d sentencing

3. From a shoebox of letters, photos, and keepsakes, I <u>gleaned</u> that my grandparents had once been young and crazy about each other.

   a guessed
   b understood
   c gathered
   d disagreed

4. Lawrence was thrilled when the judge quashed the <u>injunction</u> prohibiting him from selling the historic home.

   a stopped
   b upheld
   c reduced
   d strengthened

5. Grandma's <u>verve</u> is apparent at her famous full-moon parties.

   a sense of humor
   b vivacity
   c creepiness
   d popularity

Find an ANTONYM for each underlined word. Circle the letter of your answer.

6. Smoking had <u>blighted</u> Leslie's beautiful smile.

   a damaged

   b benefited

   c harmed

   d ruined

7. The drama club produced a <u>farce</u> about electronic communication gone haywire.

   a play

   b comedy

   c musical

   d drama

8. Ms. McCalla remained the <u>nominal</u> editor-in-chief long after she stopped being involved in day-to-day operations at the magazine.

   a actual

   b dedicated

   c devoted

   d ceremonial

9. Chuck was afraid he would be <u>ostracized</u> from/in the group once the truth about his past emerged.

   a banned

   b removed

   c included

   d suspended

10. We were the <u>recipients</u> of Alfredo's hospitality when we traveled to Guatemala.

   a donors

   b targets

   c receivers

   d guests

Choose the BEST way to complete each sentence or answer each question. Circle the letter of your answer.

11. When drivers are <u>cited</u> for traffic violations, where are they being summoned to appear?

    a   in a court of law

    b   in traffic school

    c   at the police station

    d   in small-claims court

12. The behavior of an <u>eccentric</u> is all of the following except

    a   peculiar.

    b   ordinary.

    c   odd.

    d   unusual.

13. When is a <u>posthumous</u> award given?

    a   after retirement

    b   before dinner

    c   after death

    d   before promotion

14. Susan B. Anthony was a crusader for women's <u>suffrage</u>. What right did she want?

    a   to own property

    b   to bear arms

    c   to vote

    d   to assemble

15. If you participate in a <u>foray</u>, where will you find yourself?

    a   in enemy territory

    b   at a lively party

    c   at a neighbor's home

    d   on a treacherous mission

SAT Sneak Preview

1. BLIGHT : DAMAGE : :

   (A) lend : friendship
   (B) rain : umbrella
   (C) anger : insult
   (D) joke : laughter
   (E) flavor : spice

2. Despite the nominal entry fee, Mr. Browning cited the travel expense and time away from school as — Kelly couldn't — the competition.

   (A) reasons … enter
   (B) excuses … watch
   (C) evidence … support
   (D) proof … enjoy
   (E) claims … win

3. FARCE : COMEDY : :

   (A) suspense : mystery
   (B) country : western
   (C) jazz : music
   (D) thriller : horror
   (E) art : painting

4. Major Thompson — the enemy with a foray into their — to quash the rebellion quickly and effectively.

   (A) warned … headquarters
   (B) surprised … territory
   (C) faced … strategy
   (D) welcomed … party
   (E) embraced … customs

5. Students are often shocked and amused to discover that Shakespeare's plays contain many — jokes.

   (A) ribald
   (B) serious
   (C) patient
   (D) complicated
   (E) original

Book 6, Lesson 18 Test

Find a SYNONYM for each underlined word. Circle the letter of your answer.

1. The economic advisor was an <u>adherent</u> to the philosophy of laissez-faire, so he rarely recommended intervening.

   a   follower

   b   detractor

   c   skeptic

   d   expert

2. Though her knees were knocking, Paula conducted the interview of her idol with complete <u>aplomb</u>.

   a   terror

   b   poise

   c   awkwardness

   d   professionalism

3. Tom delicately <u>broached</u> the subject of a summer abroad.

   a   sidestepped

   b   raised

   c   pondered

   d   considered

4. With practice and patience, Earl <u>surmounted</u> his phobia of public speaking.

   a   overcame

   b   accepted

   c   exercised

   d   embraced

5. Lori was <u>resplendent</u> in her wedding gown.

   a   uncomfortable

   b   acceptable

   c   pretty

   d   dazzling

Find an ANTONYM for each underlined word. Circle the letter of your answer.

6. Military authority is built on <u>adherence</u> to/from the chain of command.

    a departing

    b orders

    c sticking

    d following

7. Julia is a <u>devotee</u> of yoga.

    a enthusiast

    b practitioner

    c opponent

    d proponent

8. No matter how many times she did it, Diane was always <u>diffident</u> walking into a new classroom.

    a shy

    b confident

    c unsure

    d uneasy

9. Spot's <u>plaintive</u> stare at the empty food bowl prevented Drew from enforcing the dog's diet very long.

    a sad

    b mournful

    c happy

    d pitiful

10. Graduation <u>regalia</u> consists of a cap and gown.

    a garb

    b activity

    c costume

    d outfit

Choose the BEST way to complete each sentence or answer each question. Circle the letter of your answer.

11. To <u>brandish</u> something is an attempt to do all of the following except

    a threaten.

    b intimidate.

    c soothe.

    d menace.

12. There was an <u>extravaganza</u> when the local team won the national championship. The event was all of the following except

    a elaborate.

    b spectacular.

    c showy.

    d tame.

13. If the paper straw you are using loses its <u>integrity</u> before you finish your drink, what happens to the straw?

    a it changes color

    b it falls apart

    c it becomes stronger

    d it gets lost

14. To <u>subordinate</u> your own wants for a greater cause means to

    a make the cause more important than your wants.

    b make your wants more important than the cause.

    c work equally toward both goals.

    d choose one or the other.

15. If something is <u>tenable</u>, it is

    a believable.

    b outrageous.

    c impossible.

    d unattractive.

SAT Sneak Preview

1. To — her diffidence when speaking to a crowd, Maggie adhered to her teacher's — to "remember to breathe and smile."

    (A) show ... example

    (B) hide ... advice

    (C) reveal ... rule

    (D) relax ... dream

    (E) manage ... story

2. Thanks to his — for integrity, Jonah could make even the most — story seem tenable.

    (A) reputation ... outrageous

    (B) desire ... mundane

    (C) drive ... ordinary

    (D) need ... complicated

    (E) love ... entertaining

3. Despite the plaudits of her peers, Grace never believed that her work was —.

    (A) ordinary

    (B) acceptable

    (C) special

    (D) received

    (E) needed

4. RESPLENDENT : APPEARANCE : :

    (A) beautiful : tree

    (B) silken : pillow

    (C) sweet : sugar

    (D) spoiled : brat

    (E) delicious : flavor

5. IMPORTANCE : SUBORDINATE : :

    (A) sense : superior

    (B) age : youth

    (C) height : giant

    (D) size : building

    (E) volume : noise

Name: _____ Date: _____

Book 6, Lesson 19 Test

Find a SYNONYM for each underlined word. Circle the letter of your answer.

1. Fear of heights prevented Ryan from reaching the <u>apex</u> of the Eiffel Tower.

   a center
   b base
   c top
   d vicinity

2. During India's struggle for independence, Ghandi went on several hunger strikes and was ready to be <u>martyred</u> for the cause.

   a publicized
   b ridiculed
   c put to death
   d jailed

3. A <u>multitude</u> assembled to catch a glimpse of the candidate on her stop in town.

   a lot
   b crowd
   c group
   d demonstration

4. Placed in a glass of water, the <u>scion</u> from the philodendron should grow roots in a few weeks.

   a cutting
   b leaf
   c bud
   d bloom

5. Suzanne was happy for the chance to <u>vindicate</u> her claim that she had discovered Mark Twain's diaries.

   a promote
   b publish
   c prove
   d withdraw

Find an ANTONYM for each underlined word. Circle the letter of your answer.

6. The 21st Amendment <u>rescinded</u> the 18th Amendment, thereby ending Prohibition.

    a enforced

    b ended

    c cancelled

    d annulled

7. The family <u>revered</u> their matriarch, and they came from the four corners of the globe to celebrate her 90th birthday with her.

    a loved

    b disrespected

    c feared

    d obeyed

8. The stranger was so <u>suave</u> that everybody was immediately put at ease.

    a rude

    b smooth

    c polite

    d pleasant

9. The artist's sketch was a <u>travesty</u> of what really happened at the rally.

    a approximation

    b imitation

    c distortion

    d facsimile

10. The <u>sordid</u> facts of the bribery scandal ruined the careers of all the people involved.

    a dirty

    b pleasant

    c offensive

    d disgusting

Choose the BEST way to complete each sentence or answer each question. Circle the letter of your answer.

11. <u>Collusion</u> between businesses to artificially drive up demand for a product may be all of the following except

   a   secret.

   b   deceitful.

   c   legal.

   d   criminal.

12. <u>Indictments</u> involve what kind of charges?

   a   civil

   b   criminal

   c   credit card

   d   electrical

13. Which of the following does not have to do with <u>incinerating</u>?

   a   recycling

   b   burning

   c   fire

   d   ashes

14. The brothers' exchanges could be so <u>vitriolic</u> that strangers might think they hated each other. What element characterizes the exchanges?

   a   insults

   b   flattery

   c   sarcasm

   d   threats

15. Which of the following is not <u>judicial</u>?

   a   a judge

   b   the courts

   c   the law

   d   a senator

SAT Sneak Preview

1. INCINERATE : ASHES : :

    (A) bake : bread
    (B) blend : paint
    (C) extinguish : fire
    (D) vacuum : dust
    (E) petrify : stone

2. Although he was indicted for theft of ideas, the inventor was vindicated when his letters — that the idea was his —.

    (A) proved ... first
    (B) suggested ... also
    (C) disproved ... creation
    (D) implied ... drive
    (E) acknowledged ... inspiration

3. LAW : JUDICIAL : :

    (A) government : legislative
    (B) office : important
    (C) profession : executive
    (D) farming : agricultural
    (E) medicine : illness

4. — for refusing to reveal his sources, the reporter became a martyr for freedom of the press.

    (A) Applauded
    (B) Celebrated
    (C) Shunned
    (D) Jailed
    (E) Accepted

5. The vitriolic coverage of the sordid scandal — many of the readers so much that they — their newspaper subscriptions.

    (A) frightened ... shared
    (B) pleased ... folded
    (C) offended ... canceled
    (D) angered ... renewed
    (E) thrilled ... destroyed

Name: _____ Date: _____

Book 6, Lesson 20 Test

Find a SYNONYM for each underlined word. Circle the letter of your answer.

1. His declarations of love were clearly <u>bogus</u> since he stumbled on her name.

   a overwhelming

   b heartfelt

   c genuine

   d false

2. The <u>ascendancy</u> of the automobile meant the demise of the horse-drawn buggy.

   a revival

   b end

   c beginning

   d decline

3. Sara <u>devised</u> a plan that would allow us to visit roadside attractions along our route from Florida to Washington.

   a formed

   b outlined

   c borrowed

   d bought

4. News of Carl's delay <u>evinced</u> a frown from his grandfather.

   a displayed

   b expressed

   c provoked

   d demanded

5. Will was intimidated by the sheer weight of the <u>tome</u> assigned that week.

   a experiment

   b book

   c essay

   d problem

Find an ANTONYM for each underlined word. Circle the letter of your answer.

6. Not all decisions are <u>irrevocable</u>.

 a permanent

 b changeable

 c correct

 d unquestionable

7. <u>Martial</u> law was imposed in Hawaii after the bombing of Pearl Harbor.

 a civil

 b military

 c wartime

 d army

8. Taking pleasure in <u>mundane</u> details is key to happiness.

 a normal

 b usual

 c extraordinary

 d boring

9. Dawn <u>patronized</u> her older brother by reminding him to wear a coat and gloves.

 a insulted

 b condescended

 c belittled

 d respected

10. Several witnesses <u>refuted</u> her claim that she had never been in the restaurant before the robbery.

 a proved

 b supported

 c suggested

 d denied

Choose the BEST way to complete each sentence or answer each question. Circle the letter of your answer.

11. A <u>quirk</u> of fate is most likely to be

    a sudden.

    b predictable.

    c unremarkable.

    d uninteresting.

12. The United States sometimes uses economic <u>sanctions</u> to try to influence policy in other countries. Sanctions are

    a problems.

    b unfair.

    c actions.

    d popular.

13. Which best describes an object that is <u>enshrined</u>?

    a dangerous

    b fragile

    c worthless

    d valued

14. Which of the following is least likely to be considered <u>memorabilia</u>?

    a a Beatles poster

    b an Eisenhower campaign button

    c today's newspaper

    d a movie costume

15. A <u>querulous</u> person is most likely to

    a complain.

    b approve.

    c compliment.

    d flatter.

SAT Sneak Preview

1. — that Hank Aaron and Babe Ruth had the same —, Dad suspected that the autographed baseballs at the memorabilia show were bogus.

   (A) Convinced ... jersey
   (B) Believing ... record
   (C) Doubtful ... handwriting
   (D) Suspicious ... manager
   (E) Suspecting ... number

2. ENSHRINE : CHERISHED : :

   (A) discard : worthless
   (B) eat : hungry
   (C) console : sad
   (D) victory : triumphant
   (E) treasure : vault

3. PATRONIZE : STORE : :

   (A) admire : idol
   (B) respect : elders
   (C) train : dog
   (D) flatter : compliment
   (E) subscribe : magazine

4. Randy was so querulous that he even tried to refute Lisa's statement that grass was —.

   (A) green
   (B) delicious
   (C) poisonous
   (D) medicinal
   (E) endangered

5. Her mother refused to sanction extracurricular activities until Leigh convinced her that her schoolwork would not —.

   (A) interfere
   (B) suffer
   (C) distract
   (D) notice
   (E) improve

Book 6, Final Test 1 (Lessons 1–20)

Read the passage. Choose the BEST answer for each sentence or question about an underlined word. Circle the letter of your answer.

THE GABBY GORILLA

Koko the gorilla, a <u>scion</u> of the San Francisco Zoo's breeding program, was named Hanabi-Ko, Japanese for "fireworks child," in honor of her birth on Independence Day in 1971. Life for Koko really became exciting a year later when she met Penny Patterson, a scientist who wanted to see if the great ape could communicate. Penny had learned of the work of other researchers who had taught sign language to chimpanzees, and she believed that gorillas had the same <u>potential</u>. Koko was an able student, with both the manual <u>dexterity</u> and intellectual <u>faculties</u> needed to express herself.

Koko's vocabulary has grown to more than 1,000 signs. She has used her hands to express everything from humor and emotion to insults and moral judgment. She even <u>articulates</u> her thoughts with some signs she invented herself. The language <u>prodigy</u> also understands some 2,000 spoken words. Although she is talented at communicating with her hands, Koko still uses her voice. Apparently purring and barking remain the best way to <u>enunciate</u> her pleasure and displeasure.

Her <u>maternal</u> side began to emerge when she told Penny she wanted a kitten. She chose a gray kitten and named him "All Ball." She <u>nurtured</u> the kitten like a mother would a baby gorilla, carrying him on her back and playing with him. When she lost All Ball to a traffic accident, the sadness she <u>evinced</u> showed that gorillas experience the same basic feelings as humans. Her fans all over the world felt tremendous <u>empathy</u> for her grief.

Koko has expressed her desire to <u>propagate</u>, but she has not become a mother. To improve the chances of Koko having a baby, Penny set up a form of video dating. She showed Koko videos of different male gorillas and let Koko decide which one she liked most. She chose Ndume, and the two are good friends. Penny and the zoo hope that Koko and her companion will one day become parents. One big question the researchers would like answered is whether Koko would <u>impart</u> her ability to communicate to her child. They have seen her shaping her doll's hands into signs, and they think she would probably pass that skill along to her young.

Even if Koko never becomes the mother of a line of talking apes, she has improved the public image of her species enormously. Before Koko, gorillas were thought to be stupid, vicious brutes incapable of intelligent thought or tender emotion. Since she learned to express herself in a way humans can understand, she has set the record straight.

1. In the first paragraph, <u>dexterity</u> refers to use of

   a the head.

   b the mouth.

   c the legs.

   d the hands.

2. What types of abilities are <u>faculties</u>?

   a natural

   b learned

   c taught

   d unusual

3. As used in the second paragraph, a synonym for <u>articulates</u> is

   a says.

   b expresses.

   c writes.

   d implies.

4. Like Koko, a <u>prodigy</u> is

   a extraordinary.

   b childish.

   c common.

   d young.

5. A synonym for <u>maternal</u> is

   a playful.

   b motherly.

   c caring.

   d selfish.

6. As used in the third paragraph, <u>nurtured</u> means

   a cared for.

   b abandoned.

   c watched.

   d raised.

7. A synonym for <u>empathy</u> is

   a feeling.

   b sorrow.

   c understanding.

   d frustration.

8. As used in the fourth paragraph, <u>propagate</u> means

   a reproduce.

   b adopt.

   c grow.

   d change.

9. An antonym for <u>evinced</u> is

   a displayed.

   b showed.

   c hid.

   d expressed.

10. Which is not a synonym for <u>impart</u>?

   a give

   b bestow

   c remove

   d pass on

SAT Sneak Preview

1. In the first paragraph, <u>scion</u> most nearly means

    (A) resident
    (B) graduate
    (C) celebrity
    (D) favorite
    (E) descendant

2. In the first paragraph, <u>potential</u> most nearly means

    (A) intelligence
    (B) capacity
    (C) desire
    (D) talent
    (E) ability

3. What best captures the meaning of the word <u>enunciate</u> in the second paragraph?

    (A) describe
    (B) suggest
    (C) imply
    (D) announce
    (E) say

4. In the third paragraph, <u>evinced</u> most nearly means

    (A) expressed
    (B) felt
    (C) experienced
    (D) seemed
    (E) withheld

5. In the fourth paragraph, <u>impart</u> most nearly means

    (A) demonstrate
    (B) bestow
    (C) show
    (D) explain
    (E) take

Name: _____ Date: _____

Book 6, Final Test 2 (Lessons 1–20)

Read the passage. Choose the BEST answer for each sentence or question about an underlined word. Circle the letter of your answer.

THE PRINCE OF PEANUTS

In the early 1800s, cotton was the main cash crop in the southern United States. The textile industry had strong demand for the plant, which thrived in the rich soil and warm climate. Over time, constant planting of the same crop depreciated the nutrients in the soil. Weaker soil led to weaker crops, which led to weaker profits. By the turn of the century, southern farmers faced economic disaster. Finding the solution to a problem often requires just thinking about the problem differently. Luckily for those farmers, an agricultural scientist at the time made it his crusade to find out how to sell what would grow, rather than how to grow what would sell.

George Washington Carver was born a slave in Missouri during the Civil War. He showed a precocious talent for gardening and as a boy he was known as the "plant doctor" to friends and neighbors. He was eager to learn, but there were no local schools for black students. His drive for erudition led him to Kansas, where he graduated from high school, and then to Iowa, where he went to college to study painting and piano. His talent with plants caught the attention of Iowa State College Department of Horticulture, where he soon was the first African American student. He graduated in 1894 and became the first African American member of Iowa State's faculty that year. He gained national attention studying plant blights, and he was invited to join the faculty at Alabama's Tuskegee Institute when he finished his master's degree in 1896.

He knew that the antecedent cause of the poor soil was constant planting of cotton, which demanded nitrogen from the soil. He knew that the land needed to take a break from cotton and to grow crops that restored nitrogen, like peanuts and soybeans. He also knew that there was no demand for peanuts and soybeans. His sagacious solution was to create demand. He spent the rest of his career developing a multitude of products from the array of crops best suited to the area. He created hundreds of products from local crops, including adhesives, cheese, ink, paper, and shaving cream. It is a fallacy that Dr. Carver invented peanut butter, although he did come up with more than 300 uses for the peanut.

His work had fast, <u>tangible</u> results. Peanuts became one of the country's leading crops and created an industry worth $200 million before 1940. Of all his hundreds of discoveries, he only patented three. He <u>contended</u> that his purpose was to help the people of the community, not to profit from them. When he died in 1943, he left his life's savings to the Tuskegee Institute so that his work could continue. Southern farmers still grow cotton, but thanks to Dr. Carver's work and legacy, they no longer depend on it.

1. <u>Precocious</u> people show their abilities when they are

   a   old.

   b   relaxing.

   c   young.

   d   under pressure.

2. In the second paragraph, <u>blights</u> means

   a   seeds.

   b   diseases.

   c   blooms.

   d   roots.

3. What is a problem's <u>antecedent</u>?

   a   its cause

   b   its solution

   c   its result

   d   its complication

4. In the third paragraph, <u>sagacious</u> means

   a   bold.

   b   risky.

   c   clever.

   d   wise.

5. In this selection, <u>multitude</u> describes

   a   a large number of products.

   b   a small number of products.

   c   a stockpile of products.

   d   a demand for products.

6. A synonym for <u>array</u> is

    a   a few.

    b   a lot.

    c   a sample.

    d   a collection.

7. In the fourth paragraph, <u>contended</u> means

    a   accepted.

    b   disagreed.

    c   disputed.

    d   maintained.

8. An antonym for <u>erudition</u> is

    a   wisdom.

    b   ignorance.

    c   silliness.

    d   importance.

9. A <u>crusade</u> takes place over what period of time?

    a   instantly

    b   a little while

    c   a long time

    d   forever

10. The <u>tangible</u> nature of Dr. Carver's work means it could be

    a   touched.

    b   understood.

    c   studied.

    d   learned.

SAT Sneak Preview

1. When something is <u>depreciated</u>, its value

    (A) increases
    (B) doubles
    (C) decreases
    (D) ages
    (E) vanishes

2. In the first paragraph, <u>crusade</u> most nearly means

    (A) struggle
    (B) wish
    (C) command
    (D) hope
    (E) search

3. What best captures the meaning of the word <u>erudition</u> in the second paragraph?

    (A) freedom
    (B) knowledge
    (C) wealth
    (D) power
    (E) status

4. In the fifth paragraph, <u>fallacy</u> most nearly means

    (A) given
    (B) victory
    (C) fact
    (D) secret
    (E) wrong idea

5. In the sixth paragraph, <u>tangible</u> most nearly means

    (A) radical
    (B) significant
    (C) destructive
    (D) real
    (E) unimportant

Name: _____ Date: _____

Book 6, Final Test 3 (Lessons 1–20)

Read the passage. Choose the BEST answer for each sentence or question about an underlined word. Circle the letter of your answer.

EASY COME, EASY GO

Andrew Carnegie lived the American Dream. Born in Scotland in 1835, Carnegie and his family struggled as machines took the place of skilled labor in weaving, which was his father's trade. They came to America and settled in Pennsylvania when Carnegie was a teenager, and he soon found work in the railroad industry. He was already a rich man at 37 years old when he learned of a method for making the large quantities of steel the modern world was demanding. With wealth earned from making steel, he was able to give the world much more than building materials.

Carnegie's partner in the steel business, Henry Clay Frick, was interested in profits as well as power. He believed in running his business the way he wanted and felt that the factory workers had no right to a say in the matter. On the other hand, Carnegie had written essays in which he supported the right of workers to form unions to protect their own interests. Frick's normal response to pressure from unions was to absolutely refuse to <u>concede</u> their demands. Carnegie was interested keeping the steel moving, and during one dispute with labor, he issued Frick an <u>injunction</u> to grant the union its demands and get the workers back to the factory.

Never <u>complacent</u>, Carnegie was always looking for better ways to do things. He wanted equipment of the highest <u>caliber</u>, on the cutting edge of technology. Better machines meant fewer employees were needed, but the strong unions prevented the company from letting anyone go. This time, Carnegie told Frick to handle it however he thought best, but not to give in. Carnegie and Frick wanted to do away with the union and <u>subjugate</u> its workers. The workers not only walked out, but they also tried to stop the factory from operating with replacements. Armed guards were brought in to protect the replacement workers, and a long, violent battle resulted. In the end, the state military had to step in to return control of the factory to its owners. Carnegie had won the fight, but the damage to his reputation as a champion for labor was done.

He did not want to be known as the man who went back on his word and betrayed the working class. In his later years, he focused his energy and fortune on making the world a better place. He wanted to achieve world peace, and subsidized those institutions he felt would advance that goal. The legacy of his philanthropy is manifest in the universities, libraries, hospitals, parks, and concert halls that bear his name.

Though he donated funds for nearly 3,000 libraries, his most notable gift may be a performance hall in New York City. Carnegie Hall opened its doors in 1891 and has hosted the world's virtuoso musicians for more than a century. A performance at Carnegie Hall is considered by many to be the zenith of a career in the performing arts. Some of his other donations were considered eccentric even by those that received them. In 1904, on a tour of Princeton University's athletic facilities, he had an idea. He decided that Princeton needed a lake where students could row to take their minds off of football, a sport of which he disapproved. Two years later, there was a three-mile lake at Princeton.

By the time he died in 1919, he had given away more than $350 million. Since then, the organizations he founded have given away close to $2 billion. A quirk in his nature was that he disapproved of stockpiling wealth, yet he was the richest man of his time. He had a gift for gathering money, but it was balanced by the gifts he gave from it.

1. To concede labor's demands, Frick would have

   a ignored them.
   b granted them.
   c negotiated over them.
   d denied them.

2. In the third paragraph, caliber means

   a excellence.
   b expense.
   c value.
   d rarity.

3. An antonym for subjugate is

   a liberate.
   b enslave.
   c empower.
   d subdue.

4. A synonym for <u>subsidize</u> is

   a authorize.

   b finance.

   c plan.

   d organize.

5. In this selection, <u>virtuoso</u> describes

   a the most.

   b the least.

   c the best.

   d the worst.

6. A synonym for <u>zenith</u> is

   a edge.

   b bottom.

   c middle.

   d top.

7. In the fourth paragraph, <u>eccentric</u> means

   a odd.

   b ordinary.

   c generous.

   d unpredictable.

8. An antonym for <u>complacent</u> is

   a dissatisfied.

   b happy.

   c content.

   d curious.

9. Which is not a synonym for <u>manifest</u>?

   a apparent

   b visible

   c suggested

   d evinced

10. An antonym for <u>injunction</u> is

   a order.

   b demand.

   c request.

   d favor.

SAT Sneak Preview

1. In the second paragraph, <u>injunction</u> most nearly means

   (A) suggestion

   (B) command

   (C) threat

   (D) urge

   (E) plea

2. In the third paragraph, <u>complacent</u> most nearly means

   (A) restless

   (B) calm

   (C) worried

   (D) satisfied

   (E) anxious

3. What best captures the meaning of the word <u>manifest</u> in the fourth paragraph?

   (A) evident

   (B) hidden

   (C) suggested

   (D) implied

   (E) alive

4. In the fifth paragraph, <u>zenith</u> most nearly means

   (A) low point

   (B) beginning

   (C) end

   (D) highlight

   (E) peak

5. In the sixth paragraph, <u>quirk</u> most nearly means

    (A) peculiarity

    (B) defect

    (C) charm

    (D) element

    (E) aspect

Name: _____   Date: _____

Book 6, Final Test 4 (Lessons 1–20)

Read the passage. Choose the BEST answer for each sentence or question about an underlined word. Circle the letter of your answer.

FORM OVER FASHION

A uniform is an outfit that identifies its wearer as a member of a certain group. Police officers, package carriers, and flight attendants all wear the <u>garb</u> of their professions as a signal to the public about who they are and what can be expected of them. But not only do uniforms tell group outsiders something about group insiders, they also serve important functions within the groups. On the field of play and on the field of battle, it is crucial to be able to distinguish friend from foe. Off the field, a uniform is a boost to morale for the group that wears it. These are the primary functions for sports and military uniforms alike.

Modern military uniforms evolved as wealthy, powerful nations began to build standing armies. The <u>impetus</u> behind the decision to dress <u>militants</u> alike was as much to display that wealth and power as it was to protect and uplift the wearer. By the late 18th century, some of the world's armies wore sleeves tight enough to <u>impair</u> their musket aim and sword exercises, just for the sake of looking impressive.

The young American Revolutionary Army was much more practical. It asked that its soldiers wear a certain style of clothing, which included common things they probably already owned. They wore hunting shirts and their coats were usually brown, which was the most common color of clothing produced in the American Colonies at the time. But not having the right clothes was not a big problem, and if they needed to, they would wear whatever was available to them.

Revolutionary soldiers wore the design or color of their units on their hats. Like modern uniforms, the function of those hats was to identify members of the group. Hats were the hardest articles to come by and also the biggest source of a soldier's pride. Officers added certain <u>flamboyant</u> touches to their hats, such as feathers or buttons. These touches soon became incorporated as part of the officially <u>sanctioned</u> uniform to signify the wearer's rank and position.

The Quartermaster Corps was established on June 16, 1775, the same day that George Washington took over as Commander in Chief of the Revolutionary

Army. A quartermaster is the supply officer, and is responsible for the army's food, clothing, and equipment. The quartermaster's responsibility includes uniforms. In 1779, Congress gave the Commander in Chief the authority to decide exactly how the army should be uniformed. The things the army wears and the ways in which it wears them has become a very complicated matter since then. The quartermaster now issues newly <u>inducted</u> soldiers everything they will need, from underwear to overcoats.

There are <u>myriad</u> shoes, hats, and everything in between that are acceptable to the army. They must be worn in specific combinations depending on the job, location, and occasion if the soldier is to <u>adhere</u> to the dress code. The details are so precise that it takes more than 300 pages of instructions to cover all the rules. The army considers appearance to be an indication of discipline among its soldiers, and takes the dress code seriously. Inspecting officers subject their <u>subordinates</u> to intense <u>scrutiny</u> and <u>censure</u> those who fail to meet standards.

Modern military uniforms emphasize functionality. Today's soldiers may be called upon to serve in any climate on Earth, and their clothing needs to provide the best comfort and protection possible. Soldiers in the desert, the jungle, the tropics, the arctic, the city, and the country may look different, but the pride they feel when wearing their uniforms is the same.

1. The <u>militants</u> in the second paragraph were

   a   statesmen.
   b   fighters.
   c   poets.
   d   royalty.

2. An antonym for <u>impair</u> is

   a   weaken.
   b   maintain.
   c   improve.
   d   lessen.

3. As used in the fourth paragraph, a synonym for <u>sanctioned</u> is

   a   copied.
   b   tolerated.
   c   forbidden.
   d   approved.

4. When soldiers are <u>inducted</u>, they are

   a   admitted to service.

   b   banned from service.

   c   persuaded against service.

   d   forced into service.

5. In this selection, <u>adhere</u> means

   a   to ignore.

   b   to follow.

   c   to consider.

   d   to defy.

6. As used in the sixth paragraph, <u>subordinates</u>

   a   are under someone else's command.

   b   are free to do as they please.

   c   answer to no one.

   d   give orders.

7. A synonym for <u>censure</u> is

   a   to reward.

   b   to find fault.

   c   to praise.

   d   to disappoint.

8. Which is not a synonym for <u>garb</u>?

   a   style

   b   fabric

   c   costume

   d   outfit

9. An <u>impetus</u> is

   a   the cause of something.

   b   the result of something.

   c   the idea of something.

   d   the story of something.

10. An antonym for <u>myriad</u> is

a certain.

b unlimited.

c boundless.

d few.

SAT Sneak Preview

1. In the first paragraph, <u>garb</u> most nearly means

   (A) clothing

   (B) badge

   (C) color

   (D) haircut

   (E) trend

2. In the second paragraph, <u>impetus</u> most nearly means

   (A) excuse

   (B) history

   (C) driving force

   (D) logic

   (E) inspiration

3. What best captures the meaning of the word <u>flamboyant</u> in the third paragraph?

   (A) important

   (B) impressive

   (C) colorful

   (D) showy

   (E) frivolous

4. In the fifth paragraph, <u>myriad</u> most nearly means

   (A) various

   (B) many

   (C) few

   (D) scarce

   (E) specific

5. In the fifth paragraph, <u>scrutiny</u> most nearly means

(A) examination

(B) glances

(C) standards

(D) norms

(E) tests

Answer Key

Lesson 1 Test	Lesson 3 Test	Lesson 5 Test	Lesson 7 Test
1. B	1. D	1. D	1. B
2. A	2. A	2. C	2. D
3. C	3. C	3. A	3. A
4. A	4. C	4. B	4. D
5. A	5. D	5. D	5. A
6. D	6. A	6. A	6. A
7. A	7. A	7. D	7. A
8. B	8. C	8. C	8. D
9. D	9. B	9. A	9. D
10. C	10. B	10. A	10. B
11. C	11. D	11. B	11. A
12. A	12. A	12. A	12. A
13. C	13. C	13. D	13. B
14. A	14. D	14. C	14. C
15. C	15. A	15. A	15. D

SAT	SAT	SAT	SAT
1. E	1. B	1. C	1. D
2. A	2. A	2. A	2. A
3. C	3. D	3. E	3. C
4. B	4. D	4. D	4. B
5. D	5. C	5. B	5. D

Lesson 2 Test	Lesson 4 Test	Lesson 6 Test	Lesson 8 Test
1. D	1. D	1. B	1. C
2. C	2. A	2. A	2. A
3. A	3. D	3. B	3. D
4. A	4. C	4. A	4. A
5. D	5. B	5. D	5. B
6. C	6. D	6. B	6. B
7. A	7. A	7. C	7. B
8. B	8. C	8. C	8. A
9. D	9. A	9. B	9. D
10. D	10. B	10. A	10. A
11. A	11. C	11. C	11. D
12. D	12. A	12. C	12. C
13. B	13. A	13. A	13. A
14. A	14. A	14. B	14. B
15. C.	15. C	15. A	15. B

SAT	SAT	SAT	SAT
1. C	1. C	1. C	1. C
2. B	2. A	2. A	2. A
3. A	3. D	3. B	3. B
4. E	4. D	4. A	4. E
5. D	5. A	5. C	5. E

Answer Key

Lesson 9 Test

1. D
2. A
3. B
4. A
5. D
6. D
7. B
8. A
9. D
10. A
11. C
12. C
13. A
14. B
15. D

SAT

1. B
2. C
3. A
4. E
5. D

Lesson 10 Test

1. C
2. A
3. D
4. A
5. B
6. B
7. C
8. C
9. A
10. B
11. C
12. B
13. D
14. C
15. A

SAT

1. C
2. A
3. D
4. A
5. A

Midterm Test 1 (Lessons 1–10)

1. A
2. D
3. B
4. C
5. A
6. D
7. C
8. A
9. B
10. D

SAT

1. A
2. D
3. B
4. A
5. E

Midterm Test 2 (Lessons 1–10)

1. C
2. D
3. A
4. D
5. B
6. A
7. C
8. D
9. A
10. B

SAT

1. C
2. B
3. E
4. B
5. A

Lesson 11 Test

1. C
2. A
3. D
4. A
5. B
6. A
7. D
8. B
9. A
10. C
11. D
12. A
13. C
14. B
15. B

SAT

1. D
2. A
3. B
4. C
5. A

Lesson 12 Test

1. B
2. A
3. D
4. B
5. A
6. C
7. D
8. A
9. D
10. C
11. B
12. A
13. A
14. A
15. C

SAT

1. C
2. E
3. A
4. D
5. B

Lesson 13 Test

1. C
2. A
3. B
4. C
5. A
6. C
7. A
8. D
9. B
10. A
11. A
12. D
13. C
14. D
15. A

SAT

1. A
2. B
3. C
4. D
5. B

Lesson 14 Test

1. A
2. B
3. D
4. A
5. C
6. B
7. A
8. B
9. D
10. C
11. B
12. D
13. D
14. B
15. B

SAT

1. C
2. A
3. B
4. E
5. D

Answer Key

Lesson 15 Test

1. B
2. A
3. A
4. D
5. B
6. B
7. A
8. C
9. D
10. B
11. C
12. B
13. A
14. D
15. D

SAT

1. A
2. C
3. B
4. E
5. A

Lesson 16 Test

1. B
2. A
3. C
4. D
5. C
6. B
7. C
8. B
9. A
10. D
11. C
12. B
13. A
14. A
15. D

SAT

1. D
2. A
3. B
4. C
5. A

Lesson 17 Test

1. D
2. B
3. C
4. A
5. B
6. B
7. D
8. A
9. C
10. A
11. A
12. B
13. C
14. C
15. A

SAT

1. D
2. A
3. C
4. B
5. A

Lesson 18 Test

1. A
2. B
3. B
4. A
5. D
6. A
7. C
8. B
9. C
10. B
11. C
12. D
13. A
14. A
15. A

SAT

1. B
2. A
3. C
4. E
5. B

Lesson 19 Test

1. C
2. C
3. B
4. A
5. C
6. A
7. B
8. A
9. D
10. B
11. C
12. B
13. A
14. C
15. D

SAT

1. E
2. A
3. D
4. E
5. C

Lesson 20 Test

1. D
2. B
3. A
4. C
5. B
6. B
7. A
8. C
9. D
10. A
11. A
12. C
13. D
14. C
15. A

SAT

1. C
2. A
3. E
4. A
5. B

Final Test 1
(Lessons 1–20)

1. D
2. A
3. B
4. A
5. B
6. A
7. C
8. A
9. C
10. C

SAT

1. E
2. B
3. D
4. A
5. B

Final Test 2
(Lessons 1–20)

1. C
2. B
3. A
4. D
5. A
6. B
7. D
8. B
9. C
10. A

SAT

1. C
2. A
3. B
4. E
5. D

Answer Key

Final Test 3
(Lessons 1–20)

1. B
2. A
3. A
4. B
5. C
6. D
7. A
8. A
9. C
10. C

SAT

1. B
2. D
3. A
4. E
5. A

Final Test 4
(Lessons 1–20)

1. B
2. C
3. D
4. A
5. B
6. A
7. B
8. B
9. A
10. D

SAT

1. A
2. C
3. D
4. B
5. A